Lead the Way to Freedom

THE HEROES
Haggadah

BY RABBI KERRY OLITZKY AND RABBI DEBORAH BODIN COHEN

BEHRMAN HOUSE
www.behrmanhouse.com

Dedicated to the memories of Abraham Nathan Olitzky and Frances (Fayge) Olitzky.

—KO

Dedicated to Larry Bodin, seder leader extraordinaire.

—DBC

Editorial Consultants: Rabbi Martin S. Cohen, Erin O'Connor

Published by Behrman House, Inc., Millburn, New Jersey 07041
www.behrmanhouse.com
ISBN 978-1-68115-098-7

Recipes on pages 76-77, 79-82 used by permission of the recipe writers.
Matzo Balls by Groucho Marx originally published in Famous Recipes by Famous People (Sunset Magazine, 1940).

Illustrations adapted from the following Shutterstock.com images:
Cover: arxichtu4ki (background), ArtMari (silhouettes)
Interior: Mercury Studio IIIT, 6T, 44T, 60T, 66T (hanging green grapes), yevgeniy11 IIIT, 6T, 7BL, 44T, 45BL, 60T, 61BL,
66T, 67BL (grape leaves), Chones IV, Al Mueller V, Blue Eyes VI-VII, Arkady Mazor 1, Ukki Studio 2, Aksenova Natalya 3, barkarola
4-5 (piano), Africa Studio 5L (conductor hands), Tim UR 7BL, 45BL, 61BL, 67BL (green grapes), Mercury Studio 7BL, 45BL, 61BL,
67BL (purple grapes), Alexey Medvednikov 8-9, ArtJazz 10, Krasowit 11, Exopixel 12-13, 56-57 (broken matzah),
Derya Cakirsoy 14-15B, Paramonov Alexander 15T, Exopixel 16-17, Stephen Coburn 19, Peyker 20-21, AmVirusi 23 (Moses basket),
Artiste2d3d 23 (reeds), Potapov Alexander 24-25 (flames), Valentyn Volkov 24-25 (bush), Ian 2010 25TL, ArtMari 27, Mike H 28,
Petr Bonek 29, Kazoka 30-31T, Alexander Sviridov 31L, Mana Photo 32-33 (waves), xpixel 32-33 (sand), irin-k 34-35B,
Pavel Savchuk 34-35T, Daisy Daisy 37, Agrus 39, Tetiana Leman 40, 50-51, ElenaPhotos 41, Kuttelvaserova Stuchelova 43,
VALUA VITALY 47, Yosefus 49, Touchr 52-53, Dmitrij Skorobogatov 53BL, Iryna Denysova 54-55T, Evgeny Karandaev 55BL,
Maria Isaeva 56-57T (magnifying glass), Phish Photography 56-57T (matzah crumbs), Rawpixel.com 59, Poscreate 62BR (open
door), ziviani 62BR (stone floor), Klagyivik Viktor 62BR (night sky), Pavelr 63, Ansis Klucis 65, Alena Brozova 69, Barbara Ash 75,
Quang Ho 76, Valentina Proskurina 77, New Africa 80, P Maxwell Photography 81, PixaHub 82

Library of Congress Cataloging-in-Publication Data
Names: Olitzky, Kerry M., author. | Cohen, Deborah Bodin, 1968- author.
Title: Heroes Haggadah : lead the way to freedom / by Rabbi Kerry Olitzky and Rabbi Deborah Bodin Cohen.
Description: Millburn : Behrman House Inc, [2024] | Includes
bibliographical references and index. | Summary: "A Haggadah that
highlights the various Jewish heroes in history and the values they
exhibit as they relate to the Passover story"-- Provided by publisher.
Identifiers: LCCN 2023022549 | ISBN 9781681150987 (paperback)
Subjects: LCSH: Haggadah--Adaptations. | Seder. | Passover--Prayers and
devotions. | Heroes--Prayers and devotions.
Classification: LCC BM674.795 .O45 2024 | DDC 296.4/5371--dc23/eng/20230510
LC record available at https://lccn.loc.gov/2023022549

Illustrations by Rabbi Deborah Bodin Cohen
Design by Zahava Bogner
Edited by Dena Neusner
Recipe testing by Rebecca Neusner

Printed in China

1 3 5 7 9 8 6 4 2

CONTENTS

INTRODUCTION

"The idea that it's possible to move from slavery to freedom and from darkness to light and from despair to hope—that is the greatest Jewish story ever told."

—SHARON BROUS, FOUNDING RABBI OF IKAR

The Heroes Haggadah interprets the traditional Passover story for our generation. Tonight, let's delve into that story together. More than any other Jewish book, the traditional haggadah is continually renewed and rewritten. In each generation, our personal stories, the stories of our families, and the stories of our generation get added to it. By contributing stories of new individuals to the haggadah, we expand and add new layers of meaning to the heroic story of the Exodus. Thus, Moses, Miriam, and the Israelites are continually joined by those of each generation who do something noteworthy. These individuals help us to grow our story of freedom and liberation. We have to remember that heroes are imperfect. Yet we can still honor their achievements even when, in some cases, they didn't live a fully exemplary life.

Tonight, in the *Heroes Haggadah*, you will meet a selection of people whom we call modern Jewish heroes—some contemporary and some from the recent past. These modern heroes add to the enduring story of freedom that began with the ancient Exodus. We hope that their heroic acts will encourage dialogue and sharing around the Passover table as you retell the story of our people's miraculous journey from slavery to freedom.

Haggadah means "telling." The Jewish people have used different forms of the haggadah to tell the Passover story for perhaps as long as two thousand years. The haggadah is among the most innovative and adaptable of Jewish texts—it is as if the haggadah is perpetually unfinished and awaiting the next generation's interpretations.

There are many elements that have been added to this haggadah to enhance your seder experience. Do all of them, or pick and choose what is most meaningful to you. As you move through the haggadah, you will notice that each section is connected to a particular theme. Each section's theme is reflected in the profile of a modern hero, as well as in thought-provoking quotes and interpretative English translations of traditional Hebrew blessings. These translations highlight attributes of the Divine that reflect the haggadah's themes, capturing how human heroes partner with God in bettering our world. By recognizing and honoring these heroes, you will continue the chain of inspiration.

PREPARING FOR THE SEDER

Enjoy the seder preparations and the anticipation of an evening with family, friends, and delicious foods. Preparing for seder is part of the Passover experience, whether participants will be sitting around your table or participating remotely. If some guests are participating remotely, you may want to send a haggadah to them ahead of time or share the e-book edition with them. Modern technology gives us the unique ability to welcome remote guests around our table. Include these guests by asking them to do readings from the haggadah and encouraging them to participate in discussions.

Many of the individuals whose stories are included in this haggadah have strong memories of the anticipation that's part of this preparation. Douglas Emhoff, the first Jewish spouse of a U.S. vice president, reminisces about seder with his grandmother: "That apartment. The plastic covering on the sofa. The smell of brisket wafting in from the kitchen. And me, sitting there at the table, patiently waiting, just waiting, to dig into that delightfully gelatinous gefilte fish, which inexplicably I still love today."

The seder plate is the centerpiece of your table. There are all kinds of seder plates—from homemade, to functional and inexpensive, to handcrafted works of art. What's important is the foods placed onto the plate and the community of family and friends gathered around it.

The foods on the seder plate are symbols that help us remember the Passover story:

- **Bitter herbs** (*maror*)—usually horseradish, a reminder of the bitterness of slavery; some seder plates include a second bitter herb, called *chazeret*, which is often romaine lettuce

- ***Charoset***—a fruit and nut mixture representing the mortar used by slaves in ancient Egypt

- **Leafy greens** (*karpas*)—often parsley or celery, a symbol of springtime renewal; some people use a potato, following an old eastern European tradition developed when green vegetables were scarce

- **Shank bone** (*z'roa*)—a roasted bone, traditionally a lamb shank bone, reminiscent of animal sacrifices that our ancestors made; vegetarians sometimes use a roasted beet

- **Roasted egg** (*beitzah*)—a roasted, hard-boiled egg, symbolic of life

- **Orange**—a modern and optional addition, symbolizing the inclusion of traditionally marginalized groups

In addition, you'll need these items for your seder table:

- A plate with three pieces of matzah, under a cover
- A cup, basin, and towel for handwashing
- Extra charoset, horseradish, and parsley
- Small bowls of salt water for dipping
- Wine and grape juice
- Elijah's cup (an extra glass of wine)
- Miriam's cup (an extra glass of water)
- A haggadah for each participant
- Two candlesticks, candles, and matches
- Pillows or cushions for reclining

Lead the Way to Freedom

THE HEROES
Haggadah

A WORD OF WELCOME

Formally begin the seder by welcoming everyone and
reading aloud the following:

Heroes are not born as heroes. Everyone has the potential to
become a hero.

When an opportunity to make a difference presents itself and
one acts, that is when an everyday person can become a hero.

When a person does the right thing or advocates for change,
she can become a hero.

When a person stands up for others, he can become a hero.

When a person solves a vexing problem with ingenuity
and determination, they can become a hero.

Everyone seated around our table has the potential to
be a hero and may have even already done something
heroic. Our seder this evening will include heroes
from modern Jewish history. You may recognize some
names. Other names, you may not know. And so, as we sing the
songs of freedom, we will sing their songs, as well.

May these heroes' stories inspire us to live as our best selves
and create positive change in the world.

*"I think I'm continuing in the good tradition of many Jews
before me. I rebel against injustice."*

—ANAT HOFFMAN, ISRAELI ACTIVIST

2

CANDLE LIGHTING:
LIGHT OF FREEDOM

Tonight, we celebrate the wondrous light of freedom. Even a small spark can ignite change. As we kindle the holiday candles, we reflect on the glow left by the generations who came before us, and we dedicate ourselves to being sparks for freedom in our world.

Light the holiday candles and say these words of blessing.
On Friday night, include the words in parentheses.

בָּרוּךְ אַתָּה, יְיָ אֱלֹהֵינוּ,
מֶלֶךְ הָעוֹלָם,
אֲשֶׁר קִדְּשָׁנוּ בְּמִצְוֹתָיו
וְצִוָּנוּ לְהַדְלִיק נֵר שֶׁל
(שַׁבָּת וְשֶׁל) יוֹם טוֹב.

Baruch Atah, Adonai Eloheinu,
Melech ha'olam,
asher kid'shanu b'mitzvotav
v'tzivanu l'hadlik neir shel
(Shabbat v'shel) yom tov.

Praised are You, Holy One of Blessing, Light of the Universe, who makes us holy with mitzvot and instructs us to kindle the (Sabbath and) holiday lights.

TABLE TALK
What "sparks" can you light to change the world around you?

ORDER OF THE SEDER

Just as a musical composition requires planning, so does a seder. The order of the seder tells all the participants what to expect. Once the order is established, there is plenty of room for improvising within it.

Read or sing the order at the beginning of the seder.

FIRST CUP—*KADEISH*—קַדֵּשׁ

WASHING—*URCHATZ*—וּרְחַץ

GREENS— *KARPAS*—כַּרְפַּס

BREAKING THE MATZAH—*YACHATZ*—יַחַץ

TELLING THE STORY—*MAGGID*— מַגִּיד

WASHING AGAIN—*ROCHTZAH*—רָחְצָה

UNLEAVENED BREAD—*MOTZI MATZAH*—מוֹצִיא מַצָּה

BITTER HERBS *MAROR* מָרוֹר

HILLEL SANDWICH— *KOREICH*—כּוֹרֵךְ

THE MEAL— *SHULCHAN OREICH*—שֻׁלְחָן עוֹרֵךְ

AFIKOMAN—*TZAFUN*—צָפוּן

GIVING THANKS—*BAREICH*—בָּרֵךְ

SONGS OF PRAISE—*HALLEL*—הַלֵּל

BRINGING CLOSURE— *NIRTZAH*—נִרְצָה

MAKING A PLAN

Leonard Bernstein once said, "To achieve great things, two things are needed: a plan and not quite enough time." Bernstein certainly knew what it takes to make good music. He conducted the New York Philharmonic orchestra and composed beloved film scores, operas, and Broadway musicals like *West Side Story*. He won sixteen Grammy Awards and numerous other awards, and he also used his public presence to protest for civil rights, for peace during the Vietnam War, and against the use of nuclear weapons.

KADEISH: FIRST CUP
COMMITMENT

Fill your glass of wine or grape juice.

Tonight, with each of the four cups of wine or grape juice, we reflect on what it takes to be a hero: commitment, courage, perseverance, and vision.

Say these words, followed by the words of blessing below.
On Friday night, include the words in parentheses.

We dedicate this first cup to all those who have committed themselves to bettering our world.

בָּרוּךְ אַתָּה, יְיָ אֱלֹהֵינוּ,
מֶלֶךְ הָעוֹלָם, בּוֹרֵא פְּרִי הַגָּפֶן.

Baruch Atah, Adonai Eloheinu,
Melech ha'olam, borei p'ri hagafen.

Praised are You, Holy One of Blessing, Committed Sovereign,
who creates the fruit of the vine.

Praised are You, Holy One of Blessing, Sovereign Source of Commitment,
who makes us holy with commandments. Out of love, You have given us
(the Sabbath and) times for rejoicing, happy holidays to celebrate, and this Passover
holiday, a celebration of our freedom from slavery in Egypt. Praised are You, Holy One,
who makes holy (the Sabbath,) our community, and festivals.

בָּרוּךְ אַתָּה, יְיָ אֱלֹקֵינוּ,
מֶלֶךְ הָעוֹלָם, שֶׁהֶחֱיָנוּ, וְקִיְּמָנוּ,
וְהִגִּיעָנוּ לַזְּמַן הַזֶּה.

Baruch Atah, Adonai Eloheinu,
Melech ha'olam, shehecheyanu, v'kiy'manu,
v'higi'anu laz'man hazeh.

Praised are You, Holy One of Blessing, Sovereign of all, who has kept us alive, supported us, and helped us to reach this moment together.

Now you may drink the first of four cups of wine or grape juice.

LEADING THE WAY

Ruth Bader Ginsburg graduated at the top of her class at Columbia Law School but could not find a job because she was a woman. She did not give up, and finally a district court judge hired her as his clerk. This experience inspired Ginsburg's lifelong commitment to women's rights and creating meaningful advancements toward a more equitable, free society. Ginsburg forged her own way and then brought others along with her. Ginsburg served as a justice on the Supreme Court of the United States, only the second woman to do so.

ורחץ

URCHATZ: WASHING
RENEWAL

Water represents the potential for new beginnings. We wash our hands, or the hands of another, to remind us of the power of renewal. No matter our age, we have the potential to grow and change. We can live through tough times, renew ourselves, and move forward. When our ancestors walked through the Red Sea, they emerged as free men and women. Tonight, at this seder, we will relive their experience. How will we emerge?

Pour water from a cup or small pitcher gently over each hand into a bowl, basin, or sink. As the water washes over your hands, think about what brings you tranquility and renewal.

WATER AND THE FUEL FOR NEW DREAMS

"The water doesn't know how old you are," says Dara Torres, who, at age forty-one, was the oldest swimmer to ever earn a place on the United States Olympic team. She represented the United States in five Olympic Games and won twelve medals, the most of any Jewish athlete. It wasn't an easy path to victory. She overcame bullying, eating disorders, and injuries. Being in the water and swimming helped her heal and then renew herself and move forward. She says, "Setbacks have an upside; they fuel new dreams."

TABLE TALK
When you go through a tough time, where do you find renewal?
How do you rejuvenate yourself?

בַּרְפַּס

KARPAS: GREENS
SUSTAINABILITY

Karpas is the symbol of spring, and its presence on the seder plate reminds us of our commitment to preserve our natural world. For us to make sure that karpas is always available to us, we must protect the environment in which it grows and thrives.

Dip parsley or other greens in salt water and say:

בָּרוּךְ אַתָּה, יְיָ אֱלֹהֵינוּ,   *Baruch Atah, Adonai Eloheinu,*
מֶלֶךְ הָעוֹלָם, בּוֹרֵא פְּרִי   *Melech ha'olam, borei p'ri*
הָאֲדָמָה.   *ha'adamah.*

Praised are You, Holy One of Blessing, Sovereign of the universe, Creator of the fruit of the earth.

Now you may eat the greens.

"Every night, I go to bed with wishful dreams of that beautiful near-future post-climate-change world, and every day I wake up and work to make it happen."

—JAMIE MARGOLIN, ENVIRONMENTAL ACTIVIST

TINKERING

Simcha Blass liked to tinker. Using his engineer's mind, he hoped to make the world better through his inventions. Living on a kibbutz in the 1920s, he saw the dry, arid land around him and dreamed of fields of vegetables and orchards of fruits. How could he bring water to the desert?

Blass noticed a lush tree surrounded by smaller, struggling ones. Blass dug around the thriving tree and discovered a small leak in a water pipe under the tree's roots. The dirt protected the precious water from evaporating. Blass developed a system for placing dripping hoses close to the ground, called "drip irrigation." Today, farmers in arid places around the world use drip irrigation to grow fruits and vegetables like karpas.

YACHATZ: BREAKING THE MATZAH
WHOLENESS

Uncover the plate of matzah and break the middle
matzah into two pieces.

Wrap the larger piece, the afikoman, in a napkin.

Before dinner is complete, hide the afikoman for
the children to find later.

There is the potential for wholeness in the broken. We
break the middle matzah, then seek to find and
repair the broken piece, the afikoman.
Only then can we complete the
seder. We don't see the
middle matzah as
beyond repair. We
see an opportunity for
healing.

HEALING

Ludwig Guttmann, a German neurosurgeon, found refuge in England when the Nazis came to power. There, he revolutionized the treatment for patients with spinal cord injuries, especially wounded soldiers. Most doctors considered these patients as hopelessly broken. Guttmann, though, saw the potential for their rehabilitation through physical therapy and sports. He organized sporting competitions for his patients, which eventually evolved into the Paralympics. His progressive approach to treatment extended his patients' lives and renewed their self-respect.

מַגִּיד

MAGGID: TELLING THE STORY
HUMBLE BEGINNINGS

To retell is to relive. Tonight, we step into the experience of our ancestors, recalling the Exodus, and we make it our own. We begin with the most humble yet profound of symbols, matzah. This simple cracker, made of just wheat and water, symbolizes our hopes and commitments.

Raise the plate of matzah and say these ancient words that our ancestors have repeated for two millennia:

הָא לַחְמָא עַנְיָא דִּי אֲכָלוּ אַבְהָתָנָא
בְּאַרְעָא דְמִצְרָיִם.

Ha lachma anya di achalu avhatana b'ara d'Mitzrayim.

This is the bread of poverty that our ancestors
ate in the Land of Egypt.

Let all who are hungry come and eat.
Let all who feel broken come and celebrate with us.

Now we are here; next year may we be in the Land of Israel.

This year we are still slaves; next year may we be
truly whole and free.

ASKING GOOD QUESTIONS

When Isidor Rabi was a boy on the Lower East Side of New York, his mother greeted him after school each day with the exact same words: "Did you ask any good questions?" Rabi's mother knew the value of inquisitiveness. Nurtured to be a questioner, Rabi developed a keen interest in science, especially physics. Rabi eventually developed the technology behind MRI machines, a critical diagnostic tool in modern medicine. He received the Nobel prize for his research and, much more importantly, saved countless lives.

"This idea that you could question everything feels particularly based in my Jewish faith."

—KESHA RAM HINSDALE, STATE REPRESENTATIVE IN VERMONT

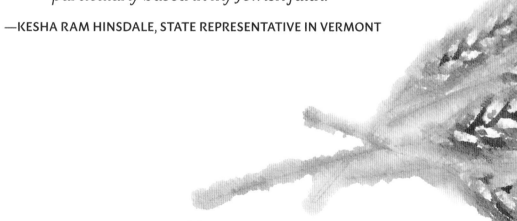

THE FOUR QUESTIONS

Ask a question. Search for an answer. Find another three questions along the way. It's the Jewish approach to life. At times, our questions and answers are one and the same. We begin our retelling of the Passover story by asking and answering the Four Questions.

~~~~~~

In many families, the youngest participant recites the Four Questions. In others, they are recited in unison.

How different is this night from all other nights!

 On all other nights, we eat either leavened bread or matzah. Tonight, why do we eat only matzah?

 On all other nights, we eat all kinds of vegetables and herbs. Tonight, why do we eat bitter herbs?

 On all other nights, we don't dip our herbs at all. Tonight, why do we dip our herbs twice?

 On all other nights, we eat either sitting up straight or reclining. Tonight, why do we recline at the table?

מַה נִּשְׁתַּנָּה הַלַּיְלָה הַזֶּה מִכָּל הַלֵּילוֹת!

1 שֶׁבְּכָל הַלֵּילוֹת אָנוּ אוֹכְלִין חָמֵץ וּמַצָּה.
הַלַּיְלָה הַזֶּה כֻּלּוֹ מַצָּה?

2 שֶׁבְּכָל הַלֵּילוֹת אָנוּ אוֹכְלִין שְׁאָר יְרָקוֹת.
הַלַּיְלָה הַזֶּה מָרוֹר?

3 שֶׁבְּכָל הַלֵּילוֹת אֵין אָנוּ מַטְבִּילִין אֲפִילוּ
פַּעַם אֶחָת. הַלַּיְלָה הַזֶּה שְׁתֵּי פְעָמִים?

4 שֶׁבְּכָל הַלֵּילוֹת אָנוּ אוֹכְלִין בֵּין יוֹשְׁבִין
וּבֵין מְסֻבִּין. הַלַּיְלָה הַזֶּה כֻּלָּנוּ מְסֻבִּין?

~~~~~~~~~~~~~~~~~~~~~~~~~~~~

Mah nishtanah halailah hazeh mikol haleilot!

1 *Sheb'chol haleilot anu och'lin chameitz umatzah.*
Halailah hazeh kulo matzah?

2 *Sheb'chol haleilot anu och'lin sh'ar y'rakot.*
Halailah hazeh maror?

3 *Sheb'chol haleilot ein anu matbilin afilu pa'am echat.*
Halailah hazeh sh'tei f'amim?

4 *Sheb'chol haleilot anu och'lin bein yosh'vin uvein m'subin.*
Halailah hazeh kulanu m'subin?

THE FOUR CHILDREN

Each person brings their own unique experiences and questions to the seder. No one approach or answer will satisfy everyone. Children's questions, especially, evolve and develop as they grow. We embrace this diversity and consider each child's needs when answering their questions.

The Wise Child asks insightful, probing questions. We respond with in-depth answers and encourage even more questions.

The Rebellious Child excludes herself from the Exodus story. We explain what the seder means to us and encourage her to see herself as part of the experience.

The Innocent Child focuses on the most basic understanding of the Exodus. We share the essentials.

The Child Who Does Not Know How to Ask does not have the words to ask a question—yet. We begin to answer while waiting for the questions to form.

FAMILY HUMOR

In the early days of movie comedy, the four Marx Brothers captured audiences' hearts with their vaudeville antics. Their popularity contributed to the acceptance of Jews in American culture. Each brother had his own unique persona on screen—Groucho was the leader, Chico was the rebel, Zeppo was the straight man, and Harpo was silent. The humor took place in watching these four very different brothers interact. Perhaps at their family seder, Groucho was the wise child, Chico was the rebellious child, Zeppo was the young child, and Harpo was the child who did not know how to ask.

TABLE TALK
Our roles constantly evolve.
This year's Wise Child might be next year's Rebel.
Who are you this year?

IN EVERY GENERATION

Recite the following phrase together aloud.
At some seders, participants sing this line over and over, for emphasis.

בְּכָל דּוֹר וָדוֹר חַיָּב אָדָם לִרְאוֹת
אֶת עַצְמוֹ כְּאִלּוּ הוּא יָצָא מִמִּצְרַיִם.

B'chol dor vador chayav adam lirot et atzmo k'ilu hu yatza miMitzrayim.

In every generation, each of us should look upon ourselves as if
we were personally freed from ancient Egypt.

Tonight, we relive the Exodus. In ancient Egypt, our Israelite ancestors toil under cruel taskmasters, and we are there. We step into the sandy footprints of the Israelite slaves and place ourselves among them. Thus, we are more fully aware of what it means to be enslaved.

Reliving their experience is the core of the seder. It reminds us that slavery did not end with the Exodus. Today, Pharaoh just takes different forms. Slavery persists through human trafficking, indentured servitude, child labor, and the use of children as soldiers. Modern slavery can also be subtle. There are people enslaved by poverty and inequality, intolerance and prejudice, ignorance, fear, and hate. We will be free only after we rid ourselves of the shackles of all forms of slavery.

PASSOVER 1979

Gershom Sizomu belongs to a small Jewish community in Uganda called Abayudaya or "Children of Judah." During Sizomu's childhood, a ruthless dictator named Idi Amin ruled Uganda. He killed many people, outlawed Judaism, and persecuted the Abayudaya. Sizomu's father was arrested for building a sukkah, and the family paid five goats to have him released. After that, Sizomu and his family stopped publicly celebrating Judaism.

On the first night of Passover in 1979, Amin was overthrown, and religious freedom was restored. Sizomu's family held a seder for two hundred people to celebrate. Sizomu grew up to be the leader of the Abayudaya. As a rabbi and member of the Ugandan parliament, he works to ensure religious freedom is never again taken away.

SLAVES IN EGYPT

Our story begins in a slave hut in ancient Egypt. A woman named Yocheved has just given birth to a baby boy. As she holds her son, Yocheved cries tears of joy, sadness, and fear, all at once. Pharaoh has recently decreed all Israelite baby boys must be killed. What will happen to her beautiful, innocent son?

Yocheved has two other children: a son named Aaron, born before Pharaoh's evil decree, and a daughter named Miriam. Yocheved devises a plan to save the baby. She waterproofs a papyrus basket with bitumen and pitch. With sad resolve, Yocheved lovingly places her son in the basket, and then she and Miriam walk to the River Nile and put the basket into the water. Yocheved turns away. She cannot watch.

Wading along the reeds at the river's edge, Miriam watches to see what will befall her brother as he floats downstream. Pharaoh's daughter, Batya, spots the basket and lifts out the baby. Miriam worries: Will the princess obey her father? Instead, as if by a miracle, Batya embraces the baby and kisses his cheek. She names him Moses and raises him in Pharaoh's palace as her own son.

TELLING STORIES

Steven Spielberg knows the keys to telling a great story: drama, emotion, compelling characters, and purpose. As a child, Spielberg used his family's home-movie camera to tell stories. He grew up to be one of the most influential movie directors of our time, telling stories like *E.T.*, *Jurassic Park*, *Saving Private Ryan*, and *Schindler's List*. His movies have helped inform and define our world.

The story of the Exodus has all the components of great drama too. Just as the best movies transport us into different worlds, tonight, our seder transports us into the Exodus story together.

TABLE TALK
In the pages ahead, we will relive Moses's story.
Think of it as a movie. If you were a filmmaker,
how would you tell it?

STANDING UP TO PHARAOH

In the palace, Moses has every privilege—the finest tutors and servants to fulfill his every request. Yet, Moses feels a deep sense of not belonging. Moses knows he was born an Israelite. He knows his people suffer in slavery.

One hot afternoon, Moses sees an Egyptian taskmaster beating an Israelite slave. Moses has witnessed the taskmasters' cruelty numerous times before. This time, he decides to act. He jumps between the taskmaster and the slave. In the scuffle, Moses kills the taskmaster. When Pharaoh hears about the incident, he is livid. How dare Moses defy him! How dare he stand up for the Israelites!

To escape Pharaoh's wrath, Moses flees into the desert. He walks many days until he happens upon a family in the land of Midian tending their flocks. The Midianites welcome Moses into their community. Instead of a prince, Moses becomes a simple shepherd.

One day, while tending a flock of sheep, Moses notices flames. A bush has caught fire. Moses looks more closely. What a curious, miraculous sight! The flames burn bright, but they don't consume the bush. As Moses approaches, he hears a voice. He knows instantly it is the voice of God: "Go back to Egypt, confront Pharaoh, and demand the Israelites' freedom. I will send your brother Aaron to help." Moses is afraid. How can he stand up to a bully as big as Pharaoh? Despite his fear, Moses agrees to return to Egypt.

24

AN UNLIKELY PRESIDENT

Volodymyr Zelensky has spent a lifetime standing up to bullies. As a boy, Zelensky grew up in a rough part of Ukraine. He refused to join the neighborhood gangs and focused on staying out of trouble. Although he trained as an attorney, Zelensky chose to pursue political comedy as a career. He used comedy to call attention to the corruption in the Ukrainian government.

Eventually, though, acting wasn't enough. Zelensky ran for and won the presidency of Ukraine on an anti-corruption platform. An unlikely victor. As president, Zelensky met his biggest bully in 2022, when Russia invaded Ukraine. Against all odds, Zelensky led his country in a valiant struggle for its freedom.

WE WERE SLAVES

Moses ventures through the barren desert toward Egypt. As he walks, he thinks about the Israelites and their dreams of freedom. For as long as he can remember, Moses has heard the Israelites sing a freedom song as they labor: "We are slaves, but one day we will be free." Moses imagines future generations singing with altered words: "*Avadim hayinu*: we were once slaves, but now we are free."

As Moses envisions the Israelites gaining their freedom, he thinks about how his own identity has changed too. He's no longer an Egyptian prince. He has reclaimed his original identity: Moses is an Israelite and a fighter for justice.

Recite or sing these words:

עֲבָדִים הָיְינוּ. עַתָּה בְּנֵי חוֹרִין.   *Avadim hayinu. Atah b'nei chorin.*

We were slaves to Pharaoh in Egypt, but God brought us out with a strong hand and an outstretched arm. Had God not brought us out of Egypt, then we and our children and our grandchildren would still be slaves.

TRANSITIONS

Abby Stein grew up as a promising yeshiva student in Brooklyn's Hasidic community. Although Stein was ordained as a Hasidic rabbi, something never felt exactly right. Stein was identified as a boy at birth but felt like a girl. In the insular Hasidic world, Stein had never heard the word transgender before secretly researching it. To transition to live as a woman, Stein had to leave the Hasidic community that had always been her home. Today, she is an activist, author, and liberal rabbi. She says that by claiming her true identity, she now has "a life worthy of celebration, not just worthy of living. It's beautiful."

TABLE TALK
Every person goes through times of transition in their lives.
What was an important time of change for you?

27

HOPE AND PROMISES

Moses walks for many days. Finally, he sees the palaces of Egypt in the distance. But another sight catches Moses's eye. It is Aaron! The brothers embrace.

Together, they walk to Pharaoh's palace. Taking a deep breath, they approach Pharaoh on the throne. Moses looks Pharaoh in the eyes and says: "Let my people go!"

The news travels quickly among the Israelites: Moses has returned. Moses's courage inspires the Israelites to believe that freedom is possible. Moses gives them hope, and from that hope comes optimism.

Raise your glass of wine or grape juice. Read or sing these words:

וְהִיא שֶׁעָמְדָה לַאֲבוֹתֵינוּ וְלָנוּ.   *V'hi she'amdah la'avoteinu v'lanu.*

The promise of freedom has been a source of strength to our ancestors and to us.

Hope can help us maintain our faith in ourselves and our community of family, friends, and neighbors. Such hope can motivate us to take action, to become heroes. Such hope can empower us to do great things, like fight for freedom and improve our nation.

Return your glass to its place, untasted.

KEEP SMILING

Kivie Kaplan grew up poor. Because he never saw his parents smile very much, he decided that smiling was one way to overcome obstacles and feel hopeful. When he saw that African Americans were still not equal In society, that didn't make him smile, so he worked hard for their rights. Eventually, he became president of the NAACP, perhaps the country's most important organization working for racial equality. And when he got older, he handed out cards to everyone he met, even President John F. Kennedy. Written on the cards were the words *Keep Smiling*.

TABLE TALK
When facing times of difficulty, what have been your
sources of strength and hope?

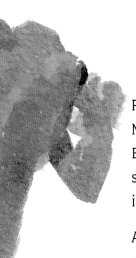

THE TEN PLAGUES

Pharaoh laughs, "Let your people go? The answer is simple: No!" Moses and Aaron do not give up. As God sends plagues into Egypt, they approach Pharaoh again and again—one, two, six, nine times—and demand freedom. Each time, Pharaoh is resolute: "No!"

After each of the first nine plagues, Pharaoh's heart is hard and he refuses to free the Israelites. Then comes the last and most terrible plague: the death of the firstborn. The last plague passes over the Israelites' homes, but they can hear the Egyptians' cries. They take no joy in the Egyptians' sufferings.

Read the list of plagues below, and dip your finger or a spoon into the glass to remove one drop of wine for each plague. We do this to lessen our joy and to acknowledge that each human life is precious.

BLOOD—*DAM*—דָּם

FROGS—*TZ'FARDEI'A*—צְפַרְדֵּעַ

LICE—*KINIM*—כִּנִּים

WILD BEASTS (OR FLIES)—*AROV*—עָרוֹב

CATTLE DISEASE—*DEVER*—דֶּבֶר

BOILS—*SH'CHIN*—שְׁחִין

HAIL—*BARAD*—בָּרָד

LOCUSTS—*ARBEH*—אַרְבֶּה

DARKNESS—*CHOSHECH*—חֹשֶׁךְ

DEATH OF THE FIRSTBORN—*MAKAT B'CHOROT*—מַכַּת בְּכוֹרוֹת

SAVING LIVES

As a boy in Greece, Albert Bourla listened to his parents talk about their experiences during the Holocaust. Their stories always ended with the same message: hate is a virus, and each human life is precious and makes a difference in our world.

Bourla studied biotechnology and found a position at the pharmaceutical giant Pfizer, researching new medicines. Just before the Covid-19 pandemic began, Bourla was promoted to lead the whole company. Faced with the worst plague in recent memory, Bourla led the scientists at Pfizer to work long hours and doubly hard to create a vaccine.

TABLE TALK
What do you consider modern-day plagues?

How can we confront these plagues
and make a difference?

"Hate is like a virus. Even accidentally, it can rapidly spread."

—JULIAN EDELMAN, FOOTBALL PLAYER

THE EXODUS

Finally, after that tenth and most terrible plague, Pharaoh agrees to free the Israelites. The Israelites pack quickly, in case Pharaoh changes his mind. They don't even wait for their bread to rise. By the light of the full moon, Moses leads them out of Egypt. For several days, they hike through the desert to the Sea of Reeds, and the border to freedom.

On the shores of the sea, the Israelites hear the thunder of chariots behind them. The Egyptians have come after them. The Israelites tremble in fear and watch as Moses raises his staff. A strong wind blows. Saltwater sprays through the air. A sandy path emerges as the sea miraculously parts. The Israelites bound forward, walking between two walls of water.

As they climb out of the seabed,
Moses sings a song of joy and
thanksgiving. Then Miriam
takes her timbrel and
leads the women
in song and dance.
They are free.

SPEAKING DIFFICULT TRUTHS

Ruth Messinger knows what it is like to stand up to those with power and influence. As Manhattan Borough President, she advocated on behalf of public schools and mediated compromise between developers and neighborhood activists. After advocating for her own community, Messinger turned her activism toward the developing world. For eighteen years, she led the American Jewish World Service, speaking out against injustice, poverty, and hate in places like Sudan, El Salvador, and Haiti.

"A hero is someone who understands the responsibility that comes with his freedom."

—BOB DYLAN, SINGER AND SONGWRITER

MIRIAM'S CUP

As you read the following, pass Miriam's cup around the table and pour a little water into it from your own water glass.

From the moment we meet the prophet Miriam in the Torah, her story is intertwined with water. As a girl, she watches over her baby brother, Moses, in the River Nile, and, as a woman, she inspires the Israelites with song and dance after crossing the Sea of Reeds. According to tradition, a miraculous source of water known as Miriam's well accompanied the Israelites in the desert, providing them with fresh water and renewing their spirit.

This Miriam's cup, filled with water, reminds us of her heroism, without which the ancient Israelites may not have survived.

SINGING HER SONG

Debbie Friedman was one of the most influential Jewish musicians and folk singers of the last century. She often incorporated the stories of Jewish women into her songs. Friedman said, "We have to reframe things so that women's voices are heard." Among her most memorable compositions was "Miriam's Song."

Her music has inspired people in packed concert halls, synagogues, and around seder tables to take timbrel in hand and get up and dance.

TABLE TALK
In the Torah, Miriam is called a prophet.
Her title highlights her wisdom and spirit.
What is a title or nickname that you've earned?
What does it mean to you?

THE RABBIS AT B'NEI B'RAK

Many years ago, in the town of B'nei B'rak, east of the modern city of Tel Aviv, five rabbis stayed up all night studying the story of the Exodus. They were so engrossed in their learning that they didn't realize the sun had risen and it was time to recite their morning prayers. Or so the story goes.

It may seem strange to include this episode in the haggadah. Some rabbis and scholars think that the story session was actually a ploy. The rabbis in B'nai B'rak may have been plotting a rebellion against the Roman authorities, who would not let them freely practice Judaism. Their students were their lookouts! Faced with Roman injustice, the rabbis had remained silent long enough.

Perhaps the story has traditionally been included in the haggadah because it reminds us that the struggle for freedom continues even after the Exodus. We cannot get complacent. When we see injustice, we need to step up and protest.

UNINTENTIONAL REBEL

Rabbi Eugene Borowitz would be among the last people whom you would expect to end up in a jail cell. A brilliant theologian and writer, Borowitz fit in far more naturally on a synagogue pulpit or in a college lecture room.

But, in 1964, Borowitz found himself spending the night in a St. Augustine jail with sixteen other rabbis and Jewish leaders. The men had gone to Florida to protest against segregation and had been arrested. At 3:00 a.m., from their cell, Borowitz wrote these words in a letter on behalf of the group. "We came because we could not stand quietly by our brother's blood. We had done that too many times before . . . silence has become the unpardonable sin of our time."

TABLE TALK

The rabbis in B'nei B'rak challenged authority because they cared about their religious freedom.

The rabbis in St. Augustine challenged authority because they cared about racial equality.

What would make you challenge authority?

ENOUGH! DAYEINU!

Whether we feel gratitude or sorrow, joy or anger, tranquility or fear, sometimes, like Moses and Miriam, we just need to sing. Like a catchy song from a Broadway musical or the beat of a rap, Dayeinu's rhythmic melody makes its theme accessible and even more piercing. How do we ever know when we have enough? How do we know that our gifts are sufficient?

~~~~~~~~~~~~~~~~~~~~~~~~~

Read or sing the following verses from Dayeinu together:

Had God brought us out of Egypt and not divided the sea for us, *dayeinu*, it would have been enough!

Had God divided the sea for us and not led us through on dry land, *dayeinu*!

Had God led us through on dry land and not nurtured us in the desert for forty years, *dayeinu*!

Had God nurtured us in the desert for forty years and not fed us manna, *dayeinu*!

Had God fed us manna and not given us Shabbat, *dayeinu*!

Had God given us Shabbat and not brought us to Mount Sinai, *dayeinu*!

Had God brought us to Mount Sinai and not given us the Torah, *dayeinu*!

Had God given us the Torah and not brought us to the Land of Israel, *dayeinu*!

Had God brought us to the Land of Israel and not built the Temple for us, *dayeinu*!

For each of these things and for all of them together, we say *dayeinu*.

אִלוּ הוֹצִיאָנוּ מִמִּצְרַיִם, דַּיֵּנוּ.

אִלוּ נָתַן לָנוּ אֶת הַשַּׁבָּת, דַּיֵּנוּ.

אִלוּ נָתַן לָנוּ אֶת הַתּוֹרָה, דַּיֵּנוּ.

Ilu hotzi'anu miMitzrayim, dayeinu.

Ilu natan lanu et haShabbat, dayeinu.

Ilu natan lanu et haTorah, dayeinu.

AN ANTIDOTE TO RACISM

Daveed Diggs found his voice by rapping. He was a poor Jewish kid of color, growing up in Oakland, California. Often people treated him differently than his white friends. It didn't stop as he grew older. Before Diggs left for New York to work on the musical *Hamilton*, a police officer threw him off his bike and against a fence because he "fit the description."

Diggs realized that when he rapped, people paid attention to his views. Rapping, and later acting and directing, became his vehicle for sharing what he saw, experienced, and believed.

TABLE TALK
Dayeinu is a song about giving thanks and showing appreciation.
What other verses would you add to it?

THE SYMBOLS ON THE TABLE

Of all the items on the seder table, the great Rabban Gamliel deemed three most essential: *pesach*, matzah, and maror. He taught that we cannot complete our seder without exploring the meaning of these three items.

~~~~~~

Point to the shank bone or beet.

Pesach—the shank bone or a beet—symbolizes an ancient Israelite offering. The Israelites marked the doorposts of their houses with the blood of a lamb on the night of the final, most terrible plague—the death of the firstborn. With this sign, the Israelites expressed their faith that this plague would spare their homes.

~~~~~~

Point to the matzah.

Matzah, or unleavened bread, symbolizes the bread of poverty—sometimes called the bread of affliction—eaten by the Israelites during the Exodus. They fled from Egypt in such a hurry that they did not have time to let their bread dough rise.

~~~~~~

Point to the horseradish (or bitter lettuce).

Maror, or bitter herbs, reminds us of how Egyptian slavery embittered the lives of Israelites.

PASSOVER ESSENTIALS

Albert Einstein, the famed physicist, made many ground-breaking discoveries, such as his theory of relativity. On Passover 1944, with war raging in Europe, Einstein embraced a different type of essential role. He felt it important to support the troops. That Passover, he attended a Jewish Welfare Board seder in Princeton, New Jersey, with young men preparing to go to war. Einstein sat at the crowded table, reading parts along with the men and lifting their spirits with his wise words. "He was not there to give a speech but to show his support for the troops," remembers Stanley Levy, who was a seventeen-year-old student and newly enlisted. "I felt blessed to be in the same room as him."

PSALMS

Language helps mold identity. In Egypt, the Israelites heard and spoke a language not their own. This was a constant reminder that they were living in a foreign land. The ancient author of the book of Psalms, who some say was King David, loved language and used words to celebrate and reflect, to mourn and to praise. This poet speaks of the Exodus as leaving "a people of strange language" then shares words of joy and thanksgiving.

~~~~~~

When Israel came forth out of Egypt,
the house of Jacob from a people of strange language,

Judah became Your sanctuary, Israel Your dominion.

The sea saw and fled; the Jordan turned backward.

The mountains skipped like rams, the hills like young sheep.

What ails you, O sea, that you flee? Jordan, that you turn backward?

You mountains, that you skip like rams; you hills, like young sheep?

Tremble, you earth, at the presence of Adonai,
at the presence of the God of Jacob;

Who turned the rock into a pool of water,
the flint into a fountain of waters.

(Psalm 114)

ANCIENT LANGUAGE ANEW

Eliezer Ben-Yehuda had a dream. For nearly two thousand years, Hebrew was used only for prayer and study. But when Ben-Yehuda moved to the Land of Israel in the late 1800s, he was determined to revive Hebrew for everyday conversations.

Ben-Yehuda spoke to everyone in Hebrew, creating new words when needed. At first, nobody could understand him. While some people believed Hebrew should remain a language just for religion, many people agreed with Ben-Yehuda and wanted to learn modern Hebrew. Ben-Yehuda reached out to the schoolteachers and taught them Hebrew. Once they began teaching Hebrew to their students, the language really took off. Because of Ben-Yehuda, Hebrew was reborn. Today, millions of people speak it.

THE SECOND CUP
COURAGE

There's a traditional story, set on the shores of the Sea of Reeds. According to this story, or midrash, when the Israelites sat trapped between Pharaoh's army and the sea waters, Moses raised his staff and nothing happened. Then a man named Nachshon stepped forward. Trembling like all the others, Nachshon walked into the sea. The water reached his knees, then his waist, then his shoulders, then his lips. Only when the water reached Nachshon's nose did the Sea of Reeds part.

This is courage.

We dedicate this second cup to all those who exhibit courage in bettering our world.

Say this blessing over the wine or grape juice:

בָּרוּךְ אַתָּה, יְיָ אֱלֹהֵינוּ, *Baruch Atah, Adonai Eloheinu,*
מֶלֶךְ הָעוֹלָם, בּוֹרֵא פְּרִי הַגָּפֶן. *Melech ha'olam, borei p'ri hagafen.*

Praised are You, Holy One of Blessing, Eternal Source of Courage, who creates the fruit of the vine.

Drink and enjoy the wine or juice.

DEFIANCE

When the Nazis invaded Poland and began rounding up Jews, Tuvia Bielski courageously vowed to fight back and save as many Jews as possible. With his brothers, he retreated to the forest and organized a resistance group that planned escape missions in the ghettos and sent scouts to guide escaping Jews to safety. The Bielski partisans are credited with building a hidden refugee community in the forest and saving hundreds of lives.

Bielski explained his mission, "We cannot simply hide ourselves. We must do something for our people. We cannot sit in the bushes and wait until the wolf comes for us. We must send people to the ghettos to save Jews."

ROCHTZAH: WASHING AGAIN
REJUVENATION

We opened our seder by washing our hands. Now we wash again, this time with a blessing. In this evening of questions, we ask: Why twice?

The first washing was practical—we cleaned our hands for the meal. This second washing is spiritual. One washing for the body, one washing for rejuvenating the soul. Tonight, we also devote body and soul to goodness and heroism.

Wash your hands again by pouring water over them, then raise them and say the words below. The phrase *n'tilat yadayim* in the blessing literally means "to raise up one's hands."

בָּרוּךְ אַתָּה, יְיָ אֱלֹהֵינוּ, מֶלֶךְ הָעוֹלָם,
אֲשֶׁר קִדְּשָׁנוּ בְּמִצְוֹתָיו וְצִוָּנוּ
עַל נְטִילַת יָדָיִם.

*Baruch Atah, Adonai Eloheinu, Melech ha'olam,
asher kid'shanu b'mitzvotav v'tzivanu
al n'tilat yadayim.*

Praised are You, Holy One of Blessing, Eternal Spirit of the Universe,
who makes us holy with mitzvot and instructs us to
ritually wash our hands.

DIGGING INTO THE PAST

A mikvah, or ritual bath, has been an essential part of Jewish community for millennia. Yigael Yadin would know. Perhaps Israel's most celebrated archaeologist, Yadin led numerous expeditions throughout Israel. He was the lead archaeologist on Masada, the ancient desert fortress that was the last Jewish stronghold against the Romans. There, Yadin's team excavated mikvah baths dating back nearly two thousand years. The ancient partisans on Masada chose to devote part of their precious rainwater to ritual purification, a kindred act to washing our hands tonight.

"If you sit on the bank of a river, you see only a small part of its surface. And yet, the water before your eyes is proof of unknowable depths."

—ANITA DIAMANT, AUTHOR AND FOUNDER OF MAYYIM HAYYIM, A MODERN MIKVAH MOVEMENT

MOTZI MATZAH: UNLEAVENED BREAD
HUMILITY

The founder of Hasidic Judaism, known as the Ba'al Shem Tov, taught that leavened bread, or *chameitz*, symbolizes self-centeredness and undue pride. Leavened bread is puffed up like an oversized ego. Matzah is different. Just flour and water, matzah is humble. On Passover, we are reminded to approach the world with humility, for only a humble person fully recognizes the needs and the humanity of others.

〜〜〜〜〜〜〜〜〜〜〜〜〜〜〜〜〜〜〜〜〜〜〜〜〜〜〜〜〜

Say these two blessings. The first one is for bread, which represents all the food that we eat. The second blessing is said just for matzah.

בָּרוּךְ אַתָּה, יְיָ אֱלֹהֵינוּ, מֶלֶךְ הָעוֹלָם,
הַמּוֹצִיא לֶחֶם מִן הָאָרֶץ.

Baruch Atah, Adonai Eloheinu, Melech ha'olam,
hamotzi lechem min ha'aretz.

Praised are You, Holy One of Blessing, Eternal Source of Nourishment,
who brings forth bread from the earth.

בָּרוּךְ אַתָּה, יְיָ אֱלֹהֵינוּ, מֶלֶךְ הָעוֹלָם,
אֲשֶׁר קִדְּשָׁנוּ בְּמִצְוֹתָיו וְצִוָּנוּ
עַל אֲכִילַת מַצָּה.

Baruch Atah, Adonai Eloheinu, Melech ha'olam,
asher kid'shanu b'mitzvotav v'tzivanu
al achilat matzah.

Praised are You, Holy One of Blessing, Eternal Provider, who makes us holy with
mitzvot and instructs us to eat matzah.

Now take your first bite of matzah. Eat it slowly and savor its taste.

THE HUMBLE STATESWOMAN

When Helen Suzman was elected to the South African Parliament in 1953, the country's apartheid laws, privileging whites and segregating Blacks, created a fundamentally unjust society. For many years, Suzman was the sole legislator in Parliament who stood against apartheid. When Suzman spoke on the parliament floor, her colleagues heckled her and drowned out her voice with antisemitic slurs.

Even when she received threatening calls and letters, Suzman didn't give up. When apartheid finally ended and Nelson Mandela was elected president of South Africa, Suzman refused to take any credit. Not "puffed up" with pride and ego, she watched joyfully from the sidelines.

"I believed in a cause—integration—and I have done something about my belief. I have tried to make my beliefs meaningful; I have not merely talked about them."

**—JUDITH FRIEZE WRIGHT,
FREEDOM RIDER IN MISSISSIPPI**

מָרוֹר

MAROR: BITTER HERBS
SORROW AND SWEETNESS

Who experienced the bitterness of Egyptian slavery? Our tradition says a "mixed multitude" of humanity left Egypt, brought together by the bitterness of shared servitude and a collective dream of freedom. We eat maror to remind ourselves of this bitterness. Without experiencing the bitterness, we can't savor the sweetness of the freedom we have.

Take a piece of horseradish or other bitter herb. Some people dip it in charoset to sweeten the taste. Then read the words below:

בָּרוּךְ אַתָּה, יְיָ אֱלֹהֵינוּ, מֶלֶךְ הָעוֹלָם,
אֲשֶׁר קִדְּשָׁנוּ בְּמִצְוֹתָיו וְצִוָּנוּ
עַל אֲכִילַת מָרוֹר.

Baruch Atah, Adonai Eloheinu, Melech ha'olam,
asher kid'shanu b'mitzvotav v'tzivanu
al achilat maror.

Praised are You, Holy One of Blessing, Source of bitter and sweet,
who makes us holy with mitzvot and instructs us to eat maror.

After you have said the words of blessing, taste the bitter herb.
Don't rush to finish it. As you chew, try to imagine the bitterness of
the lives of the ancient Israelite slaves.

KIMCHI ON THE SEDER PLATE

When Angela Warnick Buchdahl was a child, her mother put kimchi on the seder plate as their maror and as a symbol of the family's diverse identity. Buchdahl proudly celebrates both her Korean and Jewish heritage: "I grew up part of the 'mixed multitude' of our people: an Ashkenazi, Reform Jewish father, a Korean Buddhist mother." As the first Asian American cantor and rabbi, she has been a leader for ethnic diversity in Jewish leadership and Jewish life. Buchdahl's diverse background enhances, but does not define, her role as senior rabbi of Central Synagogue in New York, one of the most prominent pulpits in the United States.

TABLE TALK
What is one food or recipe that means "family"
or "memory" to you?

KOREICH: HILLEL SANDWICH
BLENDING IDENTITY

Few foods are exclusively Jewish. Rather, as our ancestors traveled the world, they ate along the way. They took local foods and made them their own. The diversity of Jewish foods represents our diverse religious and ethnic identity.

Around the world, Jews make charoset by combining the sweet tastes of the local culture, whether it be with apples and honey in the United States, bananas and dates in Iran, or mangoes and raisins in India. As charoset symbolizes the mortar of the ancient Israelites' bricks, Jewish diversity is the mortar of our community.

The ancient rabbi Hillel combined maror with charoset, lessening the bitterness of slavery with the sweetness of charoset. We continue this custom now by eating a Hillel sandwich.

~~~~~~

Distribute pieces of the bottom matzah.
Invite participants to make a matzah sandwich with maror
and charoset inside. Enjoy!

KOSHER SOUL FOOD

Award-winning food author Michael Twitty has done extensive research into food anthropology, studying how food traditions relate to identity. Twitty, who is Black, gay, and Jewish, celebrates his richly layered identity by combining the various food traditions. On his seder plate, Twitty combines molasses and pecans into charoset to "represent the gifts of the South despite its horrors in our history."

"I am Black. I am an immigrant. I am a Jew. I have an opinion. And I am not going anyplace. Get used to it."

**—NAOMI WADLER, YOUNGEST SPEAKER
AT THE MARCH FOR OUR LIVES**

שֻׁלְחָן עוֹרֵךְ

SHULCHAN OREICH: THE MEAL
ENJOYING THE BOUNTY

THE ORANGE ON THE SEDER PLATE

Many people place an orange on their seder plate. While this tradition began as a way to represent lesbian and gay inclusion in Judaism, today the orange symbolizes the fruitfulness of welcome for all those previously marginalized by the Jewish community. We eat the orange to say, "Come—all are welcome around our table. Join us."

BEGINNING THE MEAL WITH AN EGG

At this festival of spring, some families begin the meal with a simple hard-boiled egg, a symbol of life and good health that other faith traditions share. Will you dip your egg in salt water, a symbol of tears? Or in maror, a symbol of bitterness? Or perhaps in sweet charoset? Or will you eat it plain and just appreciate its simplicity?

Enjoy the meal!

EVERY SECOND OF LIFE

As a teenager in Israel, Eli Beer volunteered as an EMT. He quickly saw that ambulances had to travel long distances and sometimes arrived too late to save the patient. At the age of seventeen, Beer created a network of volunteer EMTs in his neighborhood to respond if somebody needed help nearby. The network grew to cover all of Jerusalem, then all of Israel.

Thirty years later, Beer's network has grown into United Hatzalah—six thousand volunteers treating over half a million people each year, all for free. Beer's EMTs arrive very quickly on the scene, usually within ninety seconds. Jewish, Christian, Muslim, and Druze volunteers work side by side, saving lives regardless of creed or background. The sanctity of life is all that matters. And every second counts.

צָפוּן

TZAFUN: AFIKOMAN

FINDING THE HIDDEN

Invite everyone, especially the children, to find the afikoman,
the broken matzah hidden earlier. Be prepared to offer a reward for its
return. Then break off pieces to share with everyone at the table.

We must find what is hidden—the afikoman—to complete the
seder. This can remind us: Often the greatest heroes are the
least visible. Fame, by itself, is not heroic. Heroes often do
not seek recognition. Rather they work hard, take risks, and
make sacrifices simply to do right and make a difference.

We now eat the afikoman. These final bites of the seder
meal provide us with a lasting taste of the seder experience.

A FOUND HERO

As a young woman, Regina Jonas felt a calling to be a rabbi. But Jonas was born in Germany in 1902, before women were permitted to become rabbis. She graduated from her liberal seminary with a teaching certificate but not ordination. Jonas did not give up, and finally in 1935 she was ordained. As the Nazis began arresting more prominent rabbis, Jonas took on increasing rabbinic roles of responsibility. In 1942, Jonas was deported to Theresienstadt concentration camp, where she served as a rabbi before her murder by the Nazis in October 1944.

Jonas was forgotten, and her story, like the afikoman, remained hidden until her papers were found in an obscure archive in East Berlin. Today, she is celebrated as the first female rabbi.

"We haven't really known about the countless women who have enriched our history, from biblical times on. One of the things I think feminism has brought to our society is the opportunity to discover people we've never known about."

—RABBI SALLY PRIESAND, FIRST WOMAN ORDAINED AS A RABBI IN NORTH AMERICA

BAREICH: GIVING THANKS
GRATITUDE

Gratitude is an attitude.

It can be an approach to life. More than just an appreciation for this seder night, gratitude is a lens through which we can view our daily lives—even the most routine activities.

When we are grateful for our blessings in life, it sharpens our awareness of those blessings. We are thankful for the meal we have eaten, and for the friends and family who surround us. If we delight in our time together this evening, we have the potential to feel closer to our own selves and to one another.

Fill your glass—for the third time—with grape juice or wine.
We will drink it soon. Then together repeat the following
Aramaic words. This short text from the Talmud is here in place of
the traditional blessing after meals, Birkat Hamazon.

בְּרִיךְ רַחֲמָנָא מַלְכָּא דְעָלְמָא מָרֵיהּ
דְּהִיא פִּיתָא.

B'rich rachamana malka d'alma marey d'hai pita.

Praised is the Merciful One, Eternal Provider, Creator of this bread.

PEACE, ATONEMENT, AND DIGNITY

After suffering unimaginable treatment by the Nazis during the Holocaust, Elie Wiesel transformed his pain into a life of gratitude and witness. After writing his memoir *Night*, his personal story became one of the best-known stories of the Holocaust, representing many survivors. He also became a fierce advocate for human rights, speaking out for Soviet Jews, Bosnian genocide victims, Cambodian refugees, and many others. In 1986, he received the Nobel Peace Prize for being a messenger of "peace, atonement and dignity." He once wrote: "When a person doesn't have gratitude, something is missing in his or her humanity."

TABLE TALK
What are you thankful for? Go around the table and share.

THE THIRD CUP
PERSEVERANCE

The road to improving our world is rarely straight or easy. Heroism can mean facing obstacle after obstacle until we succeed. Heroism can mean having the strength not to give up. We dedicate this third cup to heroes who have persevered against the odds.

Say this blessing:

בָּרוּךְ אַתָּה, יְיָ אֱלֹהֵינוּ,
מֶלֶךְ הָעוֹלָם, בּוֹרֵא פְּרִי הַגָּפֶן.

Baruch Atah, Adonai Eloheinu,
Melech ha'olam, borei p'ri hagafen.

Praised are You, Holy One of Blessing, Eternal Source of Perseverance, who creates the fruit of the vine.

Now you may drink the wine.

AGAINST ALL ODDS

At age three, Pnina Tamano-Shata crossed the desert in Ethiopia on foot with her five brothers and father. They found shelter at a refugee camp in Sudan and eventually were airlifted to Israel as part of Operation Moses, a rescue of nearly eight thousand Ethiopian Jews. Her mother immigrated many years later.

Once in Israel, Tamano-Shata worked hard and eventually went to law school. She pursued politics and became the first Ethiopian-born woman to serve as a member of Knesset. When Tamano-Shata was named Minister of Aliyah and Integration, she told her harrowing immigration story then pledged to work for "integration, the acceptance of the other, and against discrimination and racism."

TABLE TALK
Have you ever accomplished something that didn't come easily? What motivated you to keep trying?

ELIJAH'S CUP

Ask a participant to open the door of the house.
Then point to Elijah's cup.

This is Elijah's cup. We set aside this cup and open the door to our home to welcome Elijah the Prophet, who, according to our tradition, will announce the coming of the Messiah. We dream of a more perfect world, free from poverty, inequity, and war. It is up to us to work toward this perfected time. We begin by creating welcoming spaces in our communities and in our homes. We delight that this seder is one of those spaces.

Sing Eliyahu Hanavi, then close the door.

Elijah the prophet
Elijah the Tishbite
Elijah the Gileadite

May he come soon in our day
With the Messiah, son of David.

אֵלִיָּהוּ הַנָּבִיא,
אֵלִיָּהוּ הַתִּשְׁבִּי,
אֵלִיָּהוּ הַגִּלְעָדִי.
בִּמְהֵרָה בְיָמֵינוּ, יָבֹא אֵלֵינוּ,
עִם מָשִׁיחַ בֶּן דָּוִד.

Eliyahu hanavi
Eliyahu haTishbi
Eliyahu haGiladi.
Bimheirah v'yameinu yavo eileinu
im Mashi'ach ben David.

PROVIDING A LIFELINE

A schoolteacher in Jerusalem, Myriam Mendelow often passed poor elderly men and women panhandling. When Mendelow witnessed children taunting indigent elderly folks, her despair grew even deeper—and so did her resolve to do something. She then founded Yad LaKashish, Lifeline for the Old—a crafts center that grew quickly into an active community hub with art studios, lessons, and a gallery to sell the creations. There, the elderly found renewed purpose and made connections with scores of young volunteers. By welcoming vulnerable older adults, Mendelow helped create a more equitable, peaceful community.

"I remember opening the door for Elijah, and that was always a very special, magical moment for me. Those moments in Judaism somehow captured my imagination, those ritual moments that have to do with something mystical."

—LEONARD NIMOY, ACTOR

HALLEL: SONGS OF PRAISE
DAILY WONDERS

Nearly three thousand years ago, an ancient poet, perhaps King David, was inspired to write the holy poetry called the Psalms. When the ancient rabbis read the Psalms, they may have imagined the Israelites reciting similar poems of praise as they left Egypt. These rabbis chose their favorite psalms, the ones that best reflect the awe and mystery of our world, and called them Hallel—songs of praise. Tonight, we recite from Hallel and recognize the daily wonders that surround us.

~~~~~~~~~~~~~~~~~~~~~~~~~~~~~~~~

In the courts of Adonai's house, in your midst,
O Jerusalem.

Hallelujah.

O praise Adonai, all nations; laud God, all peoples.

For God's mercy is great toward us; and the truth of
Adonai endures forever.

Hallelujah.
(Psalms 116 and 117)

HALLELUJAH

While Leonard Cohen wrote many songs and much poetry over the course of his lifetime, he will probably be remembered best for the haunting lyrics and profound melody of his "Hallelujah." This song took nearly ten years to write and melds selections from Psalms, other biblical stories, and modern life. In "Hallelujah," Cohen captures the lament of the biblical David while, at the same time, lifting up the listener with the song's words and melody. The song has inspired countless listeners and other musicians. It has been recorded in languages as diverse as Arabic, Mandarin, French, Tagalog, and Hebrew.

"Behold I am a violin for all your songs."
—NAOMI SHEMER, ISRAELI SINGER AND SONGWRITER

THE FOURTH CUP
VISION

Heroes are often visionaries.

Dreamers imagine creative solutions. Innovators see beyond what others may accept as the norm. Doers take their dreams and innovations and make them happen. With this last cup, we offer gratitude for the ability to envision a better tomorrow, and we honor heroes who dream, innovate, and do.

Say this blessing.

בָּרוּךְ אַתָּה, יְיָ אֱלֹהֵינוּ,
מֶלֶךְ הָעוֹלָם, בּוֹרֵא פְּרִי הַגָּפֶן.

Baruch Atah, Adonai Eloheinu,
Melech ha'olam, borei p'ri hagafen.

Praised are You, Holy One of Blessing, Eternal Source of Vision,
who creates the fruit of the vine.

Now drink the wine.

HOMELAND

David Gruen may have grown up in Płońsk, Poland, but he envisioned himself as a pioneer in the Land of Israel, doing his part to create a modern nation for the Jewish people. In 1906, at the age of twenty, Gruen took the first step to fulfilling that vision: he moved to the Land of Israel while it was still under the control of the Ottomans. He took a Hebrew name, David Ben-Gurion, leaving his Diaspora identity behind. As Ben-Gurion, he worked tirelessly to lay the groundwork for an independent and self-governed country for the Jewish people. Ben-Gurion saw his vision fulfilled. On May 14, 1948, Ben-Gurion announced the State of Israel to the world and became its first prime minister.

NIRTZAH: BRINGING CLOSURE
A MORE PERFECT WORLD

Tonight, we have traveled through history, meeting heroes ancient and modern. May their examples inspire us to work toward the promise of the seder—a world of peace and freedom, where everyone values equality and treats one another with dignity and respect.

The first rabbis envisioned this more perfect world as a heavenly Jerusalem. The heroes in this haggadah had their own visions—of gender and racial equality, a clean planet, a peaceful Israel, health, prosperity, and dignity for all, as well as beautiful music, art, humor, and athletics. How do you envision it?

Together we say the following words, with the hope for a year of commitment, courage, perseverance, and vision.

לְשָׁנָה הַבָּאָה בִּירוּשָׁלָיִם! *L'shanah haba'ah biY'rushalayim!*

Next year in Jerusalem!

*"When I was a child, Israel was a legend more than a reality.
She emerged from a dream, and today she has surpassed that dream."*

**—SHIMON PERES, FORMER PRIME MINISTER OF ISRAEL,
NOBEL PEACE PRIZE LAUREATE**

TABLE TALK
Look toward the future.
What is your hope for the world?
How would you complete the sentence, "Next year. . ."?

SEDER SONGS

ECHAD MI YODEI'A: WHO KNOWS ONE?

Who knows one? I know one.
One is our God in heaven and on earth.

Who knows two? I know two.
Two are the tablets of the Covenant.
One is our God in heaven and on earth.

Who knows three? I know three.
Three are the patriarchs.
Two are the tablets of the Covenant.
One is our God in heaven and on earth.

(continue as above)

Four are the matriarchs.

Five are the books of the Torah.

Six are the sections of the Mishnah.

Seven are the days of the week.

Eight are the days to circumcision.

Nine are the months to childbirth.

Ten are the Commandments.

Eleven are the stars in Joseph's dream.

Twelve are the tribes of Israel.

Thirteen are the attributes of God.

Echad mi yodei'a? Echad ani yodei'a:
Echad Eloheinu shebashamayim uva'aretz.

Sh'nayim mi yodei'a? Sh'nayim ani yodei'a:
Sh'nei luchot habrit, echad Eloheinu
shebashamayim uva'aretz.

Sh'loshah mi yodei'a? Sh'loshah ani yodei'a:
Sh'loshah avot, sh'nei luchot habrit, echad
Eloheinu shebashamayim uva'aretz.

Arba mi yodei'a? Arba ani yodei'a:
Arba imahot, sh'loshah avot, sh'nei luchot habrit,
echad Eloheinu shebashamayim uva'aretz.

Chamishah mi yodei'a? Chamishah ani yodei'a:
Chamishah chumshei Torah, arba imahot,
sh'loshah avot, sh'nei luchot habrit, echad
Eloheinu shebashamayim uva'aretz.

Shishah mi yodei'a? Shishah ani yodei'a:
Shishah sidrei Mishnah, chamishah chumshei
Torah, arba imahot, sh'loshah avot, sh'nei luchot
habrit, echad Eloheinu shebashamayim uva'aretz.

Shivah mi yodei'a? Shivah ani yodei'a:
Shivah y'mei Shabta, shishah sidrei Mishnah,
chamishah chumshei Torah, arba imahot,
sh'loshah avot, sh'nei luchot habrit, echad
Eloheinu shebashamayim uva'aretz.

Sh'monah mi yodei'a? Sh'monah ani yodei'a:
Sh'monah y'mei milah, shivah y'mei Shabta,
shishah sidrei Mishnah, chamishah chumshei
Torah, arba imahot, sh'loshah avot, sh'nei luchot
habrit, echad Eloheinu shebashamayim uva'aretz.

אֶחָד מִי יוֹדֵעַ? אֶחָד אֲנִי יוֹדֵעַ:
אֶחָד אֱלֹהֵינוּ שֶׁבַּשָּׁמַיִם וּבָאָרֶץ.

שְׁנַיִם מִי יוֹדֵעַ? שְׁנַיִם אֲנִי יוֹדֵעַ:
שְׁנֵי לֻחוֹת הַבְּרִית.
אֶחָד אֱלֹהֵינוּ שֶׁבַּשָּׁמַיִם וּבָאָרֶץ.

שְׁלֹשָׁה מִי יוֹדֵעַ? שְׁלֹשָׁה אֲנִי יוֹדֵעַ:
שְׁלֹשָׁה אָבוֹת, שְׁנֵי לֻחוֹת הַבְּרִית.
אֶחָד אֱלֹהֵינוּ שֶׁבַּשָּׁמַיִם וּבָאָרֶץ.

(continue as above)

אַרְבַּע אִמָּהוֹת.

חֲמִשָּׁה חוּמְשֵׁי תוֹרָה.

שִׁשָּׁה סִדְרֵי מִשְׁנָה.

שִׁבְעָה יְמֵי שַׁבְּתָא.

שְׁמוֹנָה יְמֵי מִילָה.

תִּשְׁעָה יַרְחֵי לֵדָה.

עֲשָׂרָה דִּבְּרַיָּא.

אַחַד עָשָׂר כּוֹכְבַיָּא.

שְׁנַיִם עָשָׂר שִׁבְטַיָּא.

שְׁלֹשָׁה עָשָׂר מִדַּיָּא.

Tishah mi yodei'a? Tishah ani yodei'a:
Tishah yarchei leidah, sh'monah y'mei milah,
shivah y'mei Shabta, shishah sidrei Mishnah,
chamishah chumshei Torah, arba imahot,
sh'loshah avot, sh'nei luchot habrit, echad
Eloheinu shebashamayim uva'aretz.

Asarah mi yodei'a? Asarah ani yodei'a:
Asarah dibraya, tishah yarchei leidah, sh'monah
y'mei milah, shivah y'mei Shabta, shishah sidrei
Mishnah, chamishah chumshei Torah, arba
imahot, sh'loshah avot, sh'nei luchot habrit,
echad Eloheinu shebashamayim uva'aretz.

Achad asar mi yodei'a? Achad asar ani yodei'a:
Achad asar kochvaya, asarah dibraya, tishah
yarchei leidah, sh'monah y'mei milah, shivah
y'mei Shabta, shishah sidrei Mishnah, chamishah
chumshei Torah, arba imahot, sh'loshah avot,
sh'nei luchot habrit, echad Eloheinu shebashamayim uva'aretz.

Sh'neim asar mi yodei'a? Sh'neim asar ani yodei'a:
Sh'neim asar shivtaya, achad asar kochvaya,
asarah dibraya, tishah yarchei leidah, sh'monah
y'mei milah, shivah y'mei Shabta, shishah sidrei
Mishnah, chamishah chumshei Torah, arba
imahot, sh'loshah avot, sh'nei luchot habrit,
echad Eloheinu shebashamayim uva'aretz.

Sh'loshah asar mi yodei'a? Sh'loshah asar ani
yodei'a: Sh'loshah asar midaya, sh'neim asar
shivtaya, achad asar kochvaya, asarah dibraya,
tishah yarchei leidah, sh'monah y'mei milah,
shivah y'mei Shabta, shishah sidrei Mishnah,
chamishah chumshei Torah, arba imahot,
sh'loshah avot, sh'nei luchot habrit, echad
Eloheinu shebashamayim uva'aretz.

CHAD GADYA: ONE LITTLE GOAT

One little goat, one little goat, my father bought for two *zuzim, chad gadya, chad gadya*.

Then came the cat that ate the goat my father bought for two *zuzim, chad gadya, chad gadya*.

Then came the dog that bit the cat that ate the goat my father bought for two *zuzim, chad gadya, chad gadya*.

(continue as above)

Then came the stick that beat the dog . . .

Then came the fire that burned the stick . . .

Then came the water that quenched the fire . . .

Then came the ox that drank the water . . .

Then came the butcher that killed the ox . . .

Then came the angel of death that slew the butcher . . .

(final verse)

Then came the Holy One that destroyed the angel of death that slew the butcher that killed the ox that drank the water that quenched the fire that burned the stick that beat the dog that bit the cat that ate the goat my father bought for two *zuzim, chad gadya, chad gadya*.

Chad gadya, chad gadya, dizvan aba bitrei zuzei, *chad gadya, chad gadya*.

V'ata shun'ra, v'ach'lah l'gadya, dizvan aba bitrei zuzei, chad gadya, chad gadya.

V'ata chalba, v'nashach l'shun'ra, d'ach'lah l'gadya, dizvan aba bitrei zuzei, chad gadya, chad gadya.

V'ata chutra, v'hikah l'chalba, d'nashach l'shun'ra, d'ach'lah l'gadya, dizvan aba bitrei zuzei, chad gadya, chad gadya.

V'ata nura, v'saraf lchutra, d'hikah l'chalba, d'nashach l'shun'ra, d'ach'lah l'gadya, dizvan aba bitrei zuzei, chad gadya, chad gadya.

V'ata maya, v'chavah l'nura, d'saraf lchutra, d'hikah l'chalba, d'nashach l'shun'ra, d'ach'lah l'gadya, dizvan aba bitrei zuzei, chad gadya, chad gadya.

V'ata tora, v'shata l'maya, d'chavah l'nura, d'saraf lchutra, d'hikah l'chalba, d'nashach l'shun'ra, d'ach'lah l'gadya, dizvan aba bitrei zuzei, chad gadya, chad gadya.

V'ata hashocheit, v'shachat l'tora, d'shata l'maya, d'chavah l'nura, d'saraf lchutra, d'hikah l'chalba, d'nashach l'shun'ra, d'ach'lah l'gadya, dizvan aba bitrei zuzei, chad gadya, chad gadya.

V'ata malach hamavet, v'shachat l'shocheit, d'shachat l'tora, d'shata l'maya, d'chavah l'nura, d'saraf lchutra, d'hikah l'chalba, d'nashach l'shun'ra, d'ach'lah l'gadya, dizvan aba bitrei zuzei, chad gadya, chad gadya.

V'ata haKadosh Baruch Hu, v'shachat l'malach hamavet, d'shachat l'shocheit, d'shachat l'tora, d'shata l'maya, d'chavah l'nura, d'saraf lchutra, d'hikah l'chalba, d'nashach l'shun'ra, d'ach'lah l'gadya, dizvan aba bitrei zuzei, chad gadya, chad gadya.

חַד גַּדְיָא, חַד גַּדְיָא, דְּזַבֵּן אַבָּא בִּתְרֵי זוּזֵי, חַד גַּדְיָא, חַד גַּדְיָא.

וְאָתָא שׁוּנְרָא וְאָכְלָה לְגַדְיָא, דְּזַבֵּן אַבָּא בִּתְרֵי זוּזֵי, חַד גַּדְיָא, חַד גַּדְיָא.

וְאָתָא כַלְבָּא וְנָשַׁךְ לְשׁוּנְרָא, דְּאָכְלָה לְגַדְיָא, דְּזַבֵּן אַבָּא בִּתְרֵי זוּזֵי, חַד גַּדְיָא, חַד גַּדְיָא.

וְאָתָא חוּטְרָא וְהִכָּה לְכַלְבָּא, דְּנָשַׁךְ לְשׁוּנְרָא, דְּאָכְלָה לְגַדְיָא, דְּזַבֵּן אַבָּא בִּתְרֵי זוּזֵי, חַד גַּדְיָא, חַד גַּדְיָא.

וְאָתָא נוּרָא וְשָׂרַף לְחוּטְרָא, דְּהִכָּה לְכַלְבָּא, דְּנָשַׁךְ לְשׁוּנְרָא, דְּאָכְלָה לְגַדְיָא, דְּזַבֵּן אַבָּא בִּתְרֵי זוּזֵי, חַד גַּדְיָא, חַד גַּדְיָא.

וְאָתָא מַיָּא וְכָבָה לְנוּרָא, דְּשָׂרַף לְחוּטְרָא, דְּהִכָּה לְכַלְבָּא, דְּנָשַׁךְ לְשׁוּנְרָא, דְּאָכְלָה לְגַדְיָא, דְּזַבֵּן אַבָּא בִּתְרֵי זוּזֵי, חַד גַּדְיָא חַד גַּדְיָא.

וְאָתָא תוֹרָא וְשָׁתָה לְמַיָּא, דְּכָבָה לְנוּרָא, דְּשָׂרַף לְחוּטְרָא, דְּהִכָּה לְכַלְבָּא, דְּנָשַׁךְ לְשׁוּנְרָא, דְּאָכְלָה לְגַדְיָא, דְּזַבֵּן אַבָּא בִּתְרֵי זוּזֵי, חַד גַּדְיָא, חַד גַּדְיָא.

וְאָתָא הַשּׁוֹחֵט וְשָׁחַט לְתוֹרָא, דְּשָׁתָה לְמַיָּא, דְּכָבָה לְנוּרָא, דְּשָׂרַף לְחוּטְרָא, דְּהִכָּה לְכַלְבָּא, דְּנָשַׁךְ לְשׁוּנְרָא, דְּאָכְלָה לְגַדְיָא, דְּזַבֵּן אַבָּא בִּתְרֵי זוּזֵי, חַד גַּדְיָא, חַד גַּדְיָא.

וְאָתָא מַלְאַךְ הַמָּוֶת וְשָׁחַט לְשׁוֹחֵט, דְּשָׁחַט לְתוֹרָא, דְּשָׁתָה לְמַיָּא, דְּכָבָה לְנוּרָא, דְּשָׂרַף לְחוּטְרָא, דְּהִכָּה לְכַלְבָּא, דְּנָשַׁךְ לְשׁוּנְרָא, דְּאָכְלָה לְגַדְיָא, דְּזַבֵּן אַבָּא בִּתְרֵי זוּזֵי, חַד גַּדְיָא, חַד גַּדְיָא.

וְאָתָא הַקָּדוֹשׁ בָּרוּךְ הוּא וְשָׁחַט לְמַלְאַךְ הַמָּוֶת, דְּשָׁחַט לְשׁוֹחֵט, דְּשָׁחַט לְתוֹרָא, דְּשָׁתָה לְמַיָּא, דְּכָבָה לְנוּרָא, דְּשָׂרַף לְחוּטְרָא, דְּהִכָּה לְכַלְבָּא, דְּנָשַׁךְ לְשׁוּנְרָא, דְּאָכְלָה לְגַדְיָא, דְּזַבֵּן אַבָּא בִּתְרֵי זוּזֵי, חַד גַּדְיָא, חַד גַּדְיָא.

ADIR HU: GOD IS MIGHTY

God is Mighty, God is Mighty.

(Refrain)

May God build the Temple soon,
Speedily in our time, soon.
Build it, Eternal One! Build it, Eternal One!

(Repeat refrain after each line below.)

God is supreme, great, outstanding…

God is glorious, faithful, worthy…

God is kind, pure, unique…

God is mighty, wise, majestic…

God is awesome, strong, powerful…

God is redeeming, righteous, holy…

God is compassionate, almighty, resolute…

Adir hu, adir hu

(Refrain:)

Yivneh veito b'karov
bimheirah, bimheirah
b'yameinu b'karov, El b'neih, El b'neih
b'neih veit'cha b'karov.

(Repeat refrain after each line below.)

Bachur hu, gadol hu, dagul hu…

Hadur hu, vatik hu, zakai hu…

Chasid hu, tahor hu, yachid hu…

Kabir hu, lamud hu, melech hu…

Nora hu, sagiv hu, izuz hu…

Podeh hu, tzadik hu, kadosh hu…

Rachum hu, Shadai hu, takif hu…

אַדִּיר הוּא, אַדִּיר הוּא.

(Refrain)

יִבְנֶה בֵּיתוֹ בְּקָרוֹב.
בִּמְהֵרָה, בִּמְהֵרָה, בְּיָמֵינוּ בְּקָרוֹב.
אֵל בְּנֵה, אֵל בְּנֵה, בְּנֵה בֵיתְךָ בְּקָרוֹב.

(Repeat refrain after each line below.)

בָּחוּר הוּא, גָּדוֹל הוּא, דָּגוּל הוּא …

הָדוּר הוּא, וָתִיק הוּא, זַכַּאי הוּא …

חָסִיד הוּא, טָהוֹר הוּא, יָחִיד הוּא …

כַּבִּיר הוּא, לָמוּד הוּא, מֶלֶךְ הוּא …

נוֹרָא הוּא, סַגִּיב הוּא, עִזּוּז הוּא …

פּוֹדֶה הוּא, צַדִּיק הוּא, קָדוֹשׁ הוּא …

רַחוּם הוּא, שַׁדַּי הוּא, תַּקִּיף הוּא …

RECIPES

"If you preserve the food, you preserve who your family is."

—JOAN NATHAN, FOOD AUTHOR

UGANDAN CHAROSET

SIZOMU FAMILY

(PAREVE)

This charoset recipe adds an African flavor to the seder table and is traditional and familiar, and especially liked by kids. It has been adopted by the entire Abayudaya community.

Ingredients

- 2 very ripe bananas
- 2 ripe mangoes
- 2 apples
- 1 cup roasted nuts
- 1 cup kosher red wine

Directions

1. Peel the fruit and remove the mango pits and apple cores. Chop fruit into small pieces by hand or using a food processor.
2. Add the nuts and the wine and blend until smooth.

GREEK CHAROSET

RUTH MESSINGER

(PAREVE)

Ingredients

- 20 large dates, pitted and chopped
- ¾ cup walnuts, chopped
- 1 cup raisins
- ½ cup almonds
- 1 teaspoon grated lemon rind
- Sweet red wine, to taste

Directions

1. Place the dates, walnuts, raisins, almonds, and lemon rind in a food processor and process thoroughly.

2. Add wine as needed to keep the mixture swirling, and blend until it reaches a mortar-like consistency.

MATZO BALLS

GROUCHO MARX
(MEAT OR PAREVE)

A few words from Groucho on recipes: "I want to caution all of you in regards to following a recipe. It's not as simple as it might seem. For instance, I once used a recipe book to make beef stew. I boiled it for four hours, and believe it or not, it still tasted like a recipe book."

Ingredients

- 5 matzos
- 1 medium onion, finely chopped
- 4 tablespoons melted chicken fat (or canola oil)
- 1 egg
- 2 teaspoons chopped parsley
- 1 level teaspoon ground nutmeg
- Dash of salt and pepper
- 1/3 cup matzo meal
- Chicken broth to serve

Directions

1. Soak matzos in cold water, and when soft, drain and squeeze dry.

2. Brown onion in chicken fat or oil and add to matzos. Then add the egg, parsley, nutmeg, salt, and pepper, and stir until thoroughly blended.

3. Add enough matzo meal to hold contents together and roll into balls about the size of the yolk of a hard-boiled egg.

4. Place in the ice box or refrigerator for three or four hours, and when ready to serve, drop into boiling water. When they come to the top of the water, let them boil for about 30 minutes and then remove.

Originally published in *Famous Recipes by Famous People* (Sunset Magazine, 1940).

WEST AFRICAN BRISKET

MICHAEL TWITTY

(MEAT)

Ingredients

- 1 teaspoon ground ginger
- 1 tablespoon paprika
- 1 teaspoon coarse black pepper
- 1 teaspoon cinnamon
- 1 teaspoon chili powder
- 1 teaspoon cayenne pepper
- 1 tablespoon kosher salt
- One 5-pound brisket
- 4 garlic cloves, peeled and minced
- 4 tablespoons extra-virgin olive oil
- 3 onions, peeled and diced
- 3 bell peppers—green, red, and yellow—seeded and diced
- One 10-ounce can of diced tomatoes
- 1-2 tablespoons brown sugar
- 2 cups of chicken, beef, or vegetable stock
- 1 teaspoon prepared horseradish
- 2 bay leaves
- 1 sprig fresh thyme or 1 teaspoon dried thyme
- 2 large red onions, cut into rings

Instructions:

1. Preheat your oven to 325 degrees.

2. Combine the spices and salt, setting aside about two teaspoons. Sprinkle the brisket with this mixture and rub in the minced garlic. Heat three tablespoons of olive oil in a large Dutch oven or pot. Sear the beef all around. Remove from the Dutch oven and set aside.

3. Add the onion and bell pepper to the oil in the pan. Add the remaining seasoning. Sauté until the onion is translucent, then stir in the tomatoes and cook for about five minutes.

4. Add the sugar and stock, horseradish, bay leaves, and thyme.

5. Place the onion rings at the bottom and sprinkle with the remaining tablespoon of olive oil. Place the brisket on top. Cover with the vegetables and stock.

6. Cover and bake in the preheated oven for 3 1/2 hours until the brisket is fork-tender.

7. Remove the brisket, cool, and refrigerate until chilled. Remove excess fat and slice against the grain. Cover the meat with the sauce and reheat gently for half an hour or more.

MATZAH FRUIT KUGEL

JUDITH FRIEZE WRIGHT

(DAIRY OR PAREVE)

This kugel has always been part of my Passover meals. I remember it from when I was a child and my mother made it. It reminds me of loving family get-togethers, and the taste of it says "Passover" to me.

Ingredients

- 3 matzot
- 6 eggs
- ¼ cup sugar
- ½ teaspoon salt
- ¼ teaspoon cinnamon
- ½ cup raisins
- ⅓ cup chopped almonds
- 4 tart apples, shredded
- 1 grated orange rind
- 3 tablespoons cinnamon sugar, or to taste
- 3 tablespoons unsalted butter, melted, or oil

Directions

1. Preheat the oven to 350 degrees.
2. Crumple the matzot in a bowl of water and let them soak until soft. Squeeze the extra moisture out.
3. In a separate bowl, beat eggs. Add sugar, salt, and cinnamon.
4. Stir in the soaked matzah, and add raisins, almonds, shredded apple, and orange rind.
5. Put in a 1 ½-quart greased casserole dish. Sprinkle cinnamon sugar and pour melted butter over the top.
6. Bake for 45 minutes.

SYRNIKI (CHEESE PANCAKES)

ANAT HOFFMAN

(DAIRY)

My grandmother Sara Mirl Rubenstein was born in 1898 in the village of Bilgoraj, Poland. She arrived in Palestine in 1922 and was one of the founders of a new kibbutz, Ramat Rachel, in southern Jerusalem. She had many redeeming features; cooking was not one of them. However, I want to share the one delicious comfort food she made like no other. Here is her recipe for Syrniki, quintessential cheese pancakes.

Ingredients

- 1 ½ cups fresh ricotta cheese
- 3 eggs
- 2 tablespoons fine matzah meal
- 2 tablespoons potato flour
- 3 tablespoons sugar
- Dash of vanilla extract
- ¼ cup butter
- Sour cherry jam (optional)
- Sour cream (optional)

Directions

1. In a bowl, mix ricotta cheese, eggs, matzah meal, potato flour, sugar, and vanilla extract until smooth. Refrigerate for 1 hour.

2. Heat the butter in a heavy skillet and fry the pancakes for 4 to 5 minutes on each side.

3. Serve with sour cherry jam and sour cream.

CARRIBEAN COMPOTE

MICHAEL TWITTY

(PAREVE)

It's not a recipe—it's a thing...

Take equal parts of cut-up pineapple, orange, and grapefruit.

Cube it up.

Add a pinch of salt, and to taste:

Dash of cinnamon

Dash of cayenne pepper

Dash of allspice

Dash of cloves

2 tablespoons of organic sugar, raw sugar, or agave syrup, or to taste.

2 tablespoons of lemon juice, or to taste.

Stir, chill, serve.

INDEX OF HEROES

Daveed Diggs (b. 1982) is an American songwriter, rapper, and producer. Son of a Jewish mother and an African American father, he is best known for his roles as Marquis de Lafayette and Thomas Jefferson in *Hamilton*. Page 39.

Bob Dylan (b. 1941), born Robert Allen Zimmerman, is an American singer-songwriter. Some of his songs became anthems for civil rights and the anti-war movement, especially in the 1960s. He is the only songwriter to win the Nobel Prize in Literature. Page 33.

Julian Edelman (b. 1986) is a former American football player for the New England Patriots. Born to a Jewish father and a Christian mother, Edelman rediscovered his Jewish identity as an adult and regularly speaks out against antisemitism. Page 31.

Albert Einstein (1879–1955), the great German-born physicist and Nobel laureate, is best known for developing the theory of relativity. He immigrated to the United States in 1933, when Hitler came to power in Germany. Page 41.

Douglas Emhoff (b. 1964) is the first Jewish spouse of an American president or vice president. An entertainment attorney by trade, he assists his wife, Vice President Kamala Harris, with initiatives to support families. Page vi.

Debbie Friedman (1951–2011) was one of the most influential Jewish musicians of her time, bringing a highly participatory, folk-inspired musical style to synagogue prayer. She is perhaps best known for her musical version of "Mi Shebeirach," the prayer for healing. Page 35.

Ruth Bader Ginsburg (1933–2020) was the first Jewish woman to serve as a justice on the Supreme Court of the United States. Throughout her career, she championed gender equality and was lovingly referred to as the "Notorious RBG." Page 7.

Ludwig Guttmann (1899–1980), a Polish-born neurosurgeon, fled Nazi Germany and settled in England in 1939, specializing in care for paraplegics and quadriplegics. A firm believer in sports as a rehabilitation tool, he organized the Stoke Mandeville Games, the precursor to the Paralympics. Page 13.

Kesha Ram Hinsdale (b. 1986) is a member of the Vermont Senate. Born to a Jewish mother and a Hindu father, she was the youngest legislator to serve in a state-elected office when she began her political career in 2009. Her work ranges from protecting the environment to working on behalf of immigrants to ensuring fair treatment of minorities. Page 15.

Anat Hoffman (b. 1954) is an Israeli activist and one of the founders of Women of the Wall, which advocates for gender equality at the Western Wall. She served on the Jerusalem City Council for fourteen years and as executive director of the Israel Religious Action Center for twenty years. Page 2.

Regina Jonas (1902–1944), born in Germany, was the first woman ever ordained as a rabbi. She served as a rabbi in Berlin and later in the Theresienstadt concentration camp. She was murdered in Auschwitz in 1944. Page 57.

Kivie Kaplan (1904–1975) was an American businessman and philanthropist. In 1932 he joined the NAACP and served as its president from 1966 until his death. Page 29.

Jamie Margolin (b. 2001) is an American climate-justice activist and one of the founders of Zero Hour. Margolin identifies as a lesbian and speaks and writes openly about her experiences as an LGBTQ+ person. Page 10.

The Marx Brothers were an American comedy team that influenced many later comedians. The brothers were best known by their stage names: Chico/Leonard (1887–1961), Harpo/Adolph (1888–1964), Groucho/Julius (1890–1977), and Zeppo/Herbert (1901–1979). A fifth brother, Gummo/Milton (1892–1997) helped handle the business side of the act. Page 19.

Myriam Mendelow (1909-1989), an Israeli schoolteacher, founded Yad LaKashish, Lifeline for the Old, an art workshop and social services network for the elderly of Jerusalem. Page 63.

Ruth Messinger (b. 1940) served as a New York City Council member and Manhattan borough president. In 1998 she became president of American Jewish World Service, a nonprofit dedicated to human rights and global justice, and their global ambassador in 2016. Page 33.

Joan Nathan (b. 1943), an American author and journalist, has written eleven cookbooks, most on Jewish cuisine. Fans call her the "matriarch of Jewish cooking" and the "Jewish Julia Child." Page 75.

Leonard Nimoy (1931–2015) was an American actor who played the iconic character Mr. Spock in Star Trek for almost fifty years. His character was known for his Vulcan salute, inspired by Nimoy's childhood memories of the Priestly Blessing. Page 63.

Shimon Peres (1923–2016) emigrated from Poland to pre-state Israel with his family at age eleven. He served as prime minister and later as president of Israel. Along with Yitzhak Rabin and Yasser Arafat, Peres received the Nobel Peace Prize in 1994. Page 69.

Sally Priesand (b. 1946) was the first female rabbi in the world ordained by a rabbinical seminary. Her ordination took place in 1972 at Hebrew Union College-Jewish Institute of Religion in Cincinnati, Ohio. She served as rabbi of Monmouth Reform Temple in Tinton Falls, New Jersey, for twenty-five years. Page 57.

Isidor Rabi (1898–1988) won the 1944 Nobel Prize in Physics for his discovery of nuclear magnetic resonance, which is used in magnetic resonance imaging (MRI). Page 15.

Naomi Shemer (1930–2004) was a leading Israeli singer and songwriter. She is best known for her song "Yerushalayim Shel Zahav"— "Jerusalem of Gold"— which became the unofficial second anthem of Israel. Page 65.

Gershom Sizomu (b. 1972) is the first native-born Black rabbi in sub-Saharan Africa. He is the chief rabbi of the Abayudaya, the Jewish community in Uganda, and is a member of Uganda's Parliament. Page 21.

Steven Spielberg (b. 1946) is the most successful director of all time. He is known for such films as *Jaws*, *Raiders of the Lost Ark*, *ET the Extra-Terrestrial*, *Jurassic Park*, and the Academy Award-winning Holocaust film *Schindler's List*. Page 23.

Abby Stein (b. 1991), grew up in the Hasidic community and was ordained a rabbi, like generations of her ancestors before her. When she came out as transgender, she became a spokesperson for the LGBTQ+ community, began serving as a rabbi in the liberal community, and cofounded the first organization to support transgender people from the Orthodox community. Page 27.

Helen Suzman (1917–2009) served in the Parliament of South Africa for thirty-six years. An outspoken critic of apartheid, she suffered threats and verbal abuse for her views. She also received many awards and was twice nominated for the Nobel Peace Prize for her work. Page 49.

Pnina Tamano-Shata (b. 1981) immigrated to Israel from Ethiopia at age three as part of Operation Moses. A lawyer, journalist, and politician, Tamano-Shata is the first Ethiopian-born woman to serve in the Knesset. Page 61.

Dara Torres (b. 1967) is an American swimmer who competed in five Olympic Games. As the winner of twelve Olympic medals, she is the most successful Jewish Olympian of all time. Page 9.

Michael Twitty (b. 1977) is an African American-Jewish writer, culinary historian, educator, and LGBTQ+ activist. He is the author of the award-winning books *The Cooking Gene* and *Koshersoul*. Page 53.

Naomi Wadler (b. 2006) is an activist against gun violence. At age eleven, she was the youngest speaker at March for Our Lives, a demonstration in favor of gun-control legislation. Born in Ethiopia, Wadler was adopted by a Jewish family in the United States. Page 53.

Elie Wiesel (1928–2016), born in Romania, survived the Holocaust as a teenager. He wrote fifty-seven books, including *Night*, which emerged from his experience as a prisoner in Auschwitz. He received the Nobel Peace Prize in 1986 for his message of peace, atonement, and dignity. Page 59.

Judith Frieze Wright (b. 1939) is a civil rights activist. As a college student in the 1960s, she traveled to the American South with the Freedom Riders, where she joined mixed-race groups to desegregate bus stations. Page 49.

Yigael Yadin (1917–1984), an Israeli archaeologist, excavated some of the best-known sites in Israel, including the Qumran caves, Masada, Hazor, and Tel Megiddo. Yadin served as chief of staff of the Israel Defense Forces and as deputy prime minister. Page 47.

Volodymyr Zelensky (b. 1978), president of Ukraine, led the country during the Russian invasion that began in 2022. In an earlier career in television, he played the Ukrainian president in the series *Servant of the People*. Page 25.

A hero from my family or community:

_____

_____

_____

NOTES

Bernstein, p.5: Attributed to Leonard Bernstein; adapted from *The Fra*, vol. 7, 1911.

Bielski, p.45: Peter Duffy, *The Bielski Brothers* (New York: HarperCollins Publishers, 2003), 89.

Borowitz, p.37: Dr. Eugene. Borowitz "Why We Went: A Joint Letter from the Rabbis Arrested in St. Augustine." Jewish Women's Archive.

Brous, p.iv: Edgar Bronfman, *Why Be Jewish* (New York: Grand Central Publishing, 2016).

Buchdahl, p.51: Angela Buchdahl, "My Personal Story: Kimchee on the Seder Plate," *Sh'ma: A Journal of Jewish Responsibility*, (June 2003).

Diamant, p.47: Anita Diamant, *The Red Tent* (New York: St. Martin's Press, 1997).

Dylan, p.33: Steve Murphy, "Even Hard-Won Freedoms Come with Responsibility to the Greater Good." CTV News Atlantic, November 11, 2021.

Edelman, p.31: Chris Burkhardt, "Julian Edelman Pens Open Letter to Meyers Leonard Following Use of Anti-Semitic Slur." NBC Sports, March 10, 2021.

Einstein, p.41: Stanley Levy on Albert Einstein; Monica Rozenfeld, "Princeton Alumnus Remembers Passover With Einstein," *New Jersey Monthly*, April 11, 2017.

Emhoff, p.vi: Jason Hoffman and Jasmine Wright, "Second Gentleman Doug Emhoff's First Passover at the White House Brings Host of Changes to Traditional Celebration." CNN, March 26, 2021.

Hinsdale, p.15: Matthew Kassel, "She Could Be the First Jew of Color in Congress." *Jewish Insider*, January 26, 2022.

Hoffman, p.2: Anne Schuhle, "Anat Hoffman, Women of the Wall Co-Founder, to Speak in Rochester." *Democrat & Chronicle*, January 24, 2014.

Margolin, p.10: "The Day We Save Ourselves From Ourselves," quoted in Karen A. Foss, Sonja K. Foss, and Alena Amato Ruggerio, *Feminism in Practice: Communication Strategies for Making Change.* (Long Grove, IL: Waveland Press, 2021).

Nathan, p.75: Joan Nathan, *King Solomon's Table* (New York: Random House, 2017).

Nimoy, p. 63: Sonia Levitin, "A Conversation with Leonard Nimoy: The Vulcan Talks Judaism," *Reform Judaism* (Spring 1998).

Peres, p.69: Shimon Peres, "Remarks on the Occasion of His 90th Birthday," *Algemeiner*, June 19, 2013.

Priesand, p.57: Julie Zauzmer, "I Not Only Envisioned It: The First Female Rabbi Isn't Done Yet," *Washington Post*, May 24, 2016.

Shemer, p. 65: Naomi Shemer, "Yerushalayim Shel Zahav," hebrewsongs.com.

Tamano-Shata, p. 61: "The Top 100 People Positively Influencing Jewish Life, 2020." *Algemeiner*.

Torres, p 9: Dara Torres, https://www.today.com/popculture/dara-torres-there-s-no-age-limit-dreams-wbna30072528.

Wadler, p.53: Naomi Wadler, Twitter Post. July 18, 2019, 9:55 AM. https://mobile.twitter.com/naomi-wadler/status/1151852936592592897?lang=zh-Hant.

Wiesel, p. 59: Oprah Winfrey, "Oprah Talks to Elie Wiesel," *O: The Oprah Magazine*, November 2000.

Wright, p.49: Lois Daniels, "But Segregation's My Business, Too," *Boston Globe*, August 6, 1961.

Rabbi Kerry Olitzky is the author or coauthor of nearly 100 books including *Welcome to the Seder, Heroes with Chutzpah* (with coauthor Rabbi Deborah Bodin Cohen), and *Miryam's Dance*. The former executive director of Big Tent Judaism, he was named one of the fifty leading rabbis in North America by *Newsweek*. He lives in New Jersey.

Rabbi Deborah Bodin Cohen is the award-winning author of many books for children including *An Invitation to Passover* (with coauthor *Rabbi Kerry Olitzky), Nachshon Who Was Afraid to Swim*, and the Engineer Ari series. She is an editor at Behrman House and the rabbi of Congregation Beth Chai in Bethesda, Maryland.